GW00471488

OPERATION BARBAROSSA

AND THE EASTERN FRONT 1941

MICHAEL OLIVE &
ROBERT EDWARDS

Pen & Sword
MILITARY

First published in the United States of America
in 2012 by Stackpole Books

First printed in Great Britain in 2012 by
PEN & SWORD MILITARY
an imprint of
Pen & Sword Books Ltd,
47 Church Street,
Barnsley,
South Yorkshire.
S70 2AS

A CIP record for this book is available from the British Library.

ISBN 978 1 84884 867 2

Printed in the United States of America

Pen & Sword Books Ltd incorporates the Imprints of Pen & Sword Aviation,
Pen & Sword Family History, Pen & Sword Maritime, Pen & Sword Military,
Pen & Sword Discovery, Wharncliffe Local History, Wharncliffe True Crime,
Wharncliffe Transport, Pen & Sword Select, Pen & Sword Military Classics, Leo Cooper,
The Praetorian Press, Remember When, Seaforth Publishing and Frontline Publishing

For a complete list of Pen & Sword titles please contact
Pen & Sword Books Limited
47 Church Street, Barnsley, South Yorkshire, S70 2AS, England
E-mail: enquiries@pen-and-sword.co.uk
Website: www.pen-and-sword.co.uk

CONTENTS

FOREWORD

In 2003, Stackpole Books launched the Stackpole Military History Series with just two titles. Nine years on, the series continues to grow, with over 140 titles now available. Whether it's a first-person account by an American paratrooper humping through dense, light-blocking triple-canopy jungle in Vietnam, noted historians bringing new perspectives on the desperate combat between Arabs and Israelis in the Middle East, or a Swedish volunteer fighting with the Waffen SS on the Eastern Front in the Second World War, you're liable to find it in the series.

Having created a large library of the most riveting and detailed military history titles around, we started thinking about what we could do next to further explore the complex and varied history of military conflict around the globe. We strive to include strong photographs in each book, but there's only so much space for photos in a narrative history. To add to the challenge, authors don't always have a wealth of photos at their disposal. What if, I pitched to the publisher, we launched a new series that was all about the photos? What if we scoured the archives, attics, museums, and as many small and not so small privately held collections all over the world in order to bring together hundreds of photographs in each book—many never before published—to create detailed, informative,

and affordable books? Well, you're holding the answer in your hands.

Each title in the Stackpole Military Photo Series is designed as a stand-alone photographic narrative of some of the most pivotal military events in modern history. When we began to search for the perfect topic to launch the series, the mammoth and world-altering Operation Barbarossa, the German invasion of Soviet Russia on June 22, 1941, became the obvious choice. From the opening salvo, the war between Adolf Hitler's Third Reich and Joseph Stalin's Communist Russia devolved into one marked by ever-increasing acts of barbarity, fanaticism, genocide, and the wide-scale destruction of property, the environment, animals, and, above all, people.

While it might be true that a photograph is worth a thousand words, German World War II military history experts Michael Olive and Robert Edwards provide added depth and detail by illuminating every photo with engaging captions, many of them quoted directly from the soldiers themselves. Using many previously untapped sources, you'll race through humble villages and across vast steppes with the vaunted panzers, the armored fist of Germany's *blitzkrieg*. You'll see the wear and tear on men and machines as the *Wehrmacht* drives ever deeper into a Soviet Union that they fervently believe, as Hitler promised, "would come crashing down." And as winter looms, photos of German *landsers* marching across mile after mile of seemingly endless Russian steppes convey the dawning realization of these warriors that the quest for *lebensraum*—"living space"—would not be so easily acquired.

From scenes of heavy artillery lobbing shells into straw-thatched villages to pioneers braving enemy fire to construct temporary bridges over the next river in order to keep the *schwerpunkt*—"spearhead"—moving forward, *Operation Barbarossa 1941* puts you in the thick of battle. You'll witness the heroism, the fear, the fire, and the blood, all through the stark, unflinching camera lens of photographers—often soldiers themselves—standing or crouching just yards away.

As the editor for military history books at Stackpole, I am proud to welcome you to our new series. Whether you're looking for a photographic companion to a combat narrative or clear, high-resolution shots for reference for super-detailing your next model, or wanting to immerse yourself in a visual journey of ferocious combat, you'll find it here.

Chris Evans
Editor
Stackpole Books

INTRODUCTION

It had always been Hitler's intention to invade Russia, for both ideological and economic reasons. The campaign in the West, although brilliantly successful, was effectively a sideshow. Russia remained the main enemy.

Accordingly, on December 18, 1941, Hitler issued "Directive No. 21—Case Barbarossa." This directive stated:

"The German Armed Forces must be prepared, even before the conclusion of the war against England, to crush Soviet Russia in a rapid campaign ('Case Barbarossa').

"The Army will have to employ all available formations to this end, with the reservation that occupied territories must be insured against surprise attacks.

"The Air Force will have to make available for this Eastern campaign supporting forces of such strength that the Army will be able to bring land operations to a speedy conclusion . . ."[1]

The directive goes on to state that orders for the deployment would be issued eight weeks before the operation was to begin. Preparations for the invasion were to be concluded by May 15, 1941.

The intent of the operation was that the Russian Army stationed in Western Russia be destroyed by armored units penetrating deep into Russia, thereby preventing any forces from withdrawing.

It was in the "Battle of the Frontiers" where the bulk of the Russian Forces were expected to be destroyed. This was the decisive prerequisite for success: the Red Army had to be annihilated west of the line Divina-Dnieper.

The final objective of the campaign was to form a barrier from the Volga to Archangel. From this location, any surviving Russian industry located in the Urals could be eliminated by the *Luftwaffe*.

The plan of the campaign was to concentrate two powerful army groups north of the Pripet Marshes. One army group was to operate in the south with the objective of the Donets Basin and its vital industries. Moscow was to be attacked only after Army Group Center had linked up with Army Group North, advancing from East Prussia and capturing Leningrad.

At 0315 hours on Sunday, June 22, 1941, 3.6 million German and allied soldiers with 600,000 vehicles, 3,600 tanks, 7,100 artillery pieces, and 2,700 aircraft crossed the frontier. Opposing these forces were 2.9 million Soviet soldiers of the Western Military District with 15,000 tanks, 35,000 artillery pieces, and approximately 8,500 aircraft.

The front was torn apart by a massive artillery barrage followed by rapid advances of the armored and mechanized units. The Soviets were caught completely by surprise. The

Luftwaffe soon established almost complete aerial superiority, destroying hundreds of Russian aircraft on the ground in the first few hours of the attack. The Russian air force lost over 1,200 aircraft in the first eight hours of the attack.

The *Blitzkrieg* was, once again, a spectacular success. The advance on all fronts was rapid, and a number of encirclement battles ensued. The double battle of Bialystok and Minsk was concluded on July 9 with two Soviet armies being destroyed (the 3rd and the 10th) and a third (the 13th) smashed. Over 300,000 prisioners were taken; 1,400 guns and 2,500 tanks were also destroyed or captured.

The first phase of Operation Barbarossa was concluded with the capture of Smolensk on July 16. The Soviet casualties were on a par with those of the Minsk pocket. However, resistance was incredibly fierce, and the pocket was not closed until August 7. It has been convincingly argued that the battle for Smolensk effectively derailed the German Army's timetable for the capture of Moscow.

To allow the infantry divisions to close up to the moblie forces, Army Group Center was ordered, as per Directive No. 34 of July 30, to transition to the defense. Armored forces were transferred to Army Groups North and South to assist in their advances. *Panzer* generals such as Heinz Guderian argued that the mobile groups should make straight for Moscow, ignoring their flanks and leaving the mopping up of bypassed Soviet forces to the infantry divisions.

Initially, this diversion of effort seemed to be effective with the stunning German victory in the massive battle east of Kiev. The Soviet Southwest Front of Marshal Budenny was effectively destroyed, with 650,000 prisioners taken.

Hitler then agreed with his chief of staff, *General* Franz Halder, to allow Army Group Center to continue Operation Typhoon, the drive on Moscow, on September 26. However, precious time had been lost, and Russian resistance was increasing despite horrendous losses.

Once again, the German forces won an overwhelming victory as the pockets of Soviet troops west of Vyazma and Bryansk were sealed off by October 7. Resistance ended in the Vyazma pocket on October 14 and at Bryansk on October 20. Eight Soviet armies commanded by Marshal Timoshenko were detroyed and 650,000 prisioners taken. The road to Moscow seemed open.

However, the German Army in the East was nearing its limit. It was 200,000 men understrength, and no reserves were available. Tanks, guns, and vehicles were either worn out or urgently in need of maintenance. Winter was now approaching, and the few roads had become quagmires. The troops themselves were nearing exhaustion both physically and mentally. The supply situation was also critical, with tenuous, overstreched supply lines. Russian resistance also continued to show no signs of abating. This combination halted the offensive at the end of October.

When the roads froze over in November, the offensive to capture Moscow was resumed. By November 27, units of the *III Panzergruppe* had reached the Volga canal, a mere nineteen miles from the northeren outskirts of the Russian capital. German patrols had even reached the outer suburbs. All the German advances were halted on December 5, and preparations were made to retire to defensive positions for the winter. Neither of the primary objectives, Leningrad and Moscow, had been captured, and the Red Army had proved to be uncommonly resilient.

On December 6, the ruthless and canny Marshal Zhukov, commander of the central Soviet forces, launched his winter counteroffensive with fresh divisions transferred from Siberia. The almost totally unprepared Germans were then forced to fight a murderous winter battle without adequate clothing or equipment.

The final plan for Operation Barbarossa: three diverging advances to the north, center, and south. *Panzer* commanders such as Guderian, Kleist, and Hoth argued for a rapid all-out advance on Moscow, utilizing all the armored and mechanized/motorized formations.

THE GERMAN SOLDIER

For all the publicity received by the *Panzers*, it was the infantry soldier who was the backbone of the German armed forces. The early days of the campaign in Russia entailed seemingly never-ending marching, with many infantry divisions marching more than 40 kilometers per day. Infantryman Harald Harpe: "Think of the most brutal exhaustion you have ever experienced, direct burning sunlight, weeping sores on your feet—and you have my condition not at the end but at the beginning of a 45-kilometer march."[2] Despite the oppressive heat of the continental Soviet Union, most of these infantrymen still wear their heavy wool field jackets buttoned all the way up. The most variation is seen in the wearing of headgear, with most soldiers wearing their helmets, but a few marching bareheaded and one soldier in a soft cap.

The majority of the *Wehrmacht* transport was horse-drawn, not motorized, as can be seen in this instance of a *15 cm sIG 33* infantry gun team (*schweres Infanterie-Geschütz 33* — Heavy Infantry Gun, Model 33). In fact, the Red Army had far more motorized transport for its elements.

A squad of battle-weary but proud infantry pose for a group photo with a captured Soviet flag. For the infantry, Operation Barbarossa became a monotonous series of marches over great distances interspersed with combat against an often poorly led but formidable and tenacious foe. Unlike previous campaigns in Poland, the Low Countries, France, and the Balkans, the prospects for a quick and decisive victory in Russia bled away as summer turned to autumn and the first snows appeared.

An *MG 34* machine-gun team. The lightweight *MG 34*, with its high rate of fire, was vastly superior to the bulky Russian Maxim. However, the weapon was complex and expensive to produce, eventually being replaced by the exceptional *MG 42*, which was largely machine-stamped in production, versus the machine-tooling employed with much of the *MG 34*.

Motorized and mechanized units spearheaded the advance, with the hard-marching infantry striving to fill the gap.

A supply convoy on one of Russia's better roads—until the autumn rain turns it into a sea of mud. Due to the lack of transport capacity, trucks were usually reserved for supplies, and the infantry had to advance on foot. It was relatively rare to find roads with improved surfaces. Bridges were likewise Spartan and had limited load capacity, which was geared to the normal traffic it was expected to bear. Obviously, this posed problems for motorized columns and often necessitated the building of auxiliary bridges or extensive reinforcement of existing spans.

Russia has numerous wide rivers and streams that seriously impeded the German advance. In this instance, the infantry are preparing to cross a river on an inflatable raft that could also be used to support a small bridge. A forced river crossing was always a risky and difficult operation. As can be seen in this image, even a weak defensive force would be capable of impeding a crossing, given the naturally defensible terrain at its disposal.

Although not of the highest quality, this photograph illustrates the wide variety of transport used by the German army. In addition to the logistical problems created by an army that was largely resupplied by horse-drawn transport, the available motorized transport came from a wide variety of sources, including captured stocks from defeated and occupied countries.

A fine study of a rider and his constant companion. Horses were sometimes able to negotiate difficult terrain more easily than tracked vehicles and were particularly useful for reconnaissance. German horse-mounted cavalry formations were employed until the end of the war, and the reconnaissance elements of infantry divisions were often on horseback.

One area where the Germans had a marked advantage over the Russians was command and control. Russian communications were totally inadequate in the initial period of the war. In this instance, a radio team is using a *Torn. Fu.d2* high-frequency radio transmitter with a voice-transmission range of 2 miles (3.2 kilometers). Morse code transmissions usually went at least twice as far, and all radio operators, who were school trained, were required to master Morse code. Despite its relatively large size, this was considered a backpack radio set.

An observation post set up in a forward area and manned by two enlisted personnel. The field gear includes a mess kit, canteen, gas mask canister, entrenching tool, and an *M 35* dispatch case. The stripes on the soldiers' shoulder straps either represent some sort of unit identification marker or indicate that the two are officer candidates.

Judging by the equipment being carried, this is not a patrol but a working party possibly setting up a forward obsrvation/communication post. This image may have been taken in the northern part of the Soviet Union, since all of the men are wearing mosquito masks—mosquitos were particularly vexing in the northern regions of the country.

A well-equipped infantry officer wearing binoculars and an *MP40* submachine gun discusses the next action. The *Wehrmacht* went to great lengths to train junior officers to take the initiative and to deviate from set battle plans when necessary in order to achieve the objective. This meant leading from the front, which resulted in a high loss rate among these men.

The mechanized myth of the *Blitzkrieg* and the horse-drawn reality. The significantly different speeds of most German formations compared to the motorized and *Panzer* divisions were a major problem. Of the 108 infantry divisions available at the start of Barbarossa, only 13 were motorized. Of those 13 divisions, few were actually mechanized in the modern sense of the word. Of the two motorized rifle regiments in each division, it was rare for there to be more than one company with *Schützenpanzerwagen* (armored personnel carriers).

Motorcycle troops—*Kradschützen*—essental for forward scouting/reconnaissance. Often these daring riders would operate far ahead of the advancing troops. Motorcycle infantry battalions were present in each of the motorized and armored divisions. They had been invaluable in the initial campaigns of the war in western Europe, where there was an extensive network of improved roads, but their effectiveness was often impacted in Russia, where the lack of improved roads—indeed, any type of roads—slowed them, especially in rainy seasons and winter. By the spring of 1943, most of the motorcycle infantry battalions were consolidated with the divisional reconnaissance battalions and the motorcycles were traded in for light or medium half-tracks.

Captured Russian weapons being inspected—in this instance a DP light machinegun, the standard light automatic weapon of the Red Army. The circular magazine held forty-seven rounds. It was a hardy and reliable weapon.

The 1910 version of the Maxim machine gun, the SPM. It was a cumbersome weapon with a rate of fire of 500 rounds per minute. Captured weapons were issued to German garrison and coastal defense forces.

The *Wehrmacht* equivalent of the Maxim: the *MG 34*, used here in the light machine-gun role. The rate of fire was a staggering (for the time) 900 rounds per minute. The *MG 34* was the first multipurpose, selective-fire machine gun.

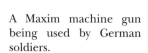

A Maxim machine gun being used by German soldiers.

The ever-present danger: "Attention!! Mines. Keep to the road." The Soviets were masters of minefield emplacement. German soldiers often complained that hasty minefields were emplaced right in front of their positions at night without their outposts ever noticing it.

The advance continues through a devastated buitlt-up area. A Russian civilian, W. F. Romanowskij, was in Minsk during the fighting in 1941 and noted: "Burning houses, debris, and ruins. Bodies lay in the streets all around."[3]

A superb photograph of a German enlisted man with maps and a general-purpose field telephone, the *Feldfernsprecher 33*. The soldier is most likely a messenger, given the logbooks and notebooks near the telephone.

A Russian village burns in the distance while an infantry squad takes cover in a farm field. An NCO scans their next objective, no doubt searching for signs of the Red Army. The panzers were tasked with large, sweeping movements meant to get deep behind the Soviet lines in order to encircle entire armies, which meant bypassing small pockets of resistance. This task fell to the infantry, who, while often appearing to be alone in photographs, could in fact count on support from the *Luftwaffe* and, to a much greater degree, the artillery.

Continuous marching, dust, and burning buildings. The seemingly tireless infantry plod on.

Is the soldier at the front looking at a map or reading a newspaper? It has been claimed that you could even sleep while on the march! Soldier exhaustion in combat is a constant problem for leadership, regardless of the army, and extra guards often had to be posted by the Germans to ensure that resting soldiers would be awakened on schedule or the guard force itself did not fall asleep on duty.

Despite the victories gained and the vast distances of the advances into the Russian heartland, the Red Army continued to resist fiercely. While the *Panzers* advanced, it was up to the infantry to consolidate those gains and repel counterattacks. During the encirclement battles, the infantry units were also the vital second ring containing the trapped enemy formations. Of interest in this image is the use of a "procured" cart for transporting the heavier items of equipment issued to an element. These carts were universally referred to by the German soldier as *panje* carts. A *panje* was the small but tough Russian packhorse used to move these carts.

The fifth soldier from the right is carrying a mine detector, indicating this might be an engineer unit on mine-clearing duty. Two soldiers are carrying probes in the form of long poles with metal tips. The tips were pushed into the ground to make contact with buried mines in order to mark and then remove them.

The German Army began Barbarossa with 625,000 horses and about 600,000 motor vehicles. The death rates of these pack animals were enormous, particularly during the harsh winters, when feed was in even shorter supply than normal.

Waffen SS troops of a communications unit laying field telephone cable. At the beginning of the war in the East, the *Waffen SS* was not a numerically strong force, and there were only about six divisions or division equivalents fielded. By the end of the war, the *Waffen SS* numbered some 560,000 men under arms, a nearly fivefold increase from 1941.

Waffen SS firing a 7.5cm *leIG 18*, a light infantry gun intended to give infantry regiments immediate fire support. The 13th Company of each infantry regiment was an infantry gun company.

The *Waffen SS* were pioneers in the use of camouflage. In both of these photographs, the soldiers are wearing camouflage smocks and helmet covers over the standard field uniform.

Reconnaissance troops of *Leibstandarte SS Adolf Hitler* enter a burning Russian town.

Waffen SS troops supporting an army assault gun unit. During Barbarossa the *Waffen SS* units were under direct army command, as they were for most of the war.

A mountain unit prepares for a rail movement. The soldiers are finishing mounting machine guns on a dual *Flak* mount. The soldiers can be identified as mountain troopers by their footgear and caps. Although the German Army later introduced a billed field cap for universal wear—the *M 43*—the only soldiers sporting a billed field cap in Barbarossa were mountain forces. Moreover, this cap can be differentiated from the *M 43* by the shorter bill. The rail car belonged to the marshaling yards of the Reichsbahn in Stuttgart and has nothing to do with the unit or its garrison location.

A powered assault craft races across a waterway. Given the number of waterways in the Soviet Union, the demand for these and non-powered assault craft was high. The powered craft tended to be used in deliberate river crossings, where there was little need for surprise, since the enemy was already aware that a crossing attempt was going to be forced. On the other hand, non-powered craft were favored for hasty crossings, in which the enemy was to be taken by surprise. Non-powered craft were also used during deliberate crossings in order to ferry assault engineers and troops across the waterway in advance of the main assault and artillery preparation in order to put breaching teams ashore undetected.

Waffen SS soldiers line up in formation. Several carry machine-gun ammunition canisters, while others are outfitted with entrenching tools.

A *Luftwaffe Flak* unit equipped with the 2cm *Flak 38*. This weapon was, along with the 3.7cm *Flak 36*, the standard light antiaircraft gun of the German armed forces.

Army soldiers of the elite *Infanterie-Regiment (mot) "Großdeutschland"* enjoy some down time while awaiting rail movement. The soldiers can be identified as having been assigned to *"Großdeutschland"* by the intertwined *DG* cipher on their shoulder straps and the wearing of *"Großdeutschland"* cuff title on their right sleeve. Because of the sleeve band, members of this formation are often mistaken for the *Waffen SS*. The regiment later grew to divisional status and is rightly considered one of the elite formations of the German Army during the war.

A near miss: a shell impacts in no-man's-land.

Rounds impact in the water, probably in the northern theater of operations along the Baltic. Depite a lack of armored and mechanized formations, Army Group North advanced rapidly, but was not strong enough to capture Leningrad. The decision was then made to lay siege to the city and starve the defenders into surrender.

A staging area for captured Soviet materiel and prisoners. Scenes such as this were common in the opening stages of Barbarossa.

Stretcher-bearers carry a wounded comrade across open terrain. Medics usually wore Red Cross armbands and helmet covers, so these may have been frontline soldiers impressed into stretcher-bearer duty to help with overflow.

Personnel tend to wounded on a horse-drawn medic wagon. Serious cases were usually evacuated to troop-clearing facilities by means of motorized vehicles or even aircraft, while the "walking wounded" were triaged this way.

A wounded man is evacuated from a field ambulance while an officer and senior noncommissioned officer supervise. One of the personnel helping evacuate the wounded man does not appear to be a German, based on his headgear and other details of his uniform. He might be a *Hilfsfreiwilliger*—"volunteer helper"—one of many Russian soldiers who surrendered to the advancing German forces and then volunteered to be auxiliaries rather than go to a prison camp.

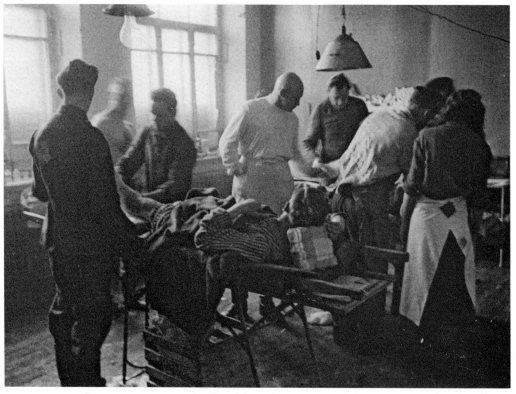

An operating room in a field hospital. This appears to be one farther removed from the front lines, as one of the assistants is female and female nurses were not allowed in the combat zone.

Life in the rear areas was not always so harsh or devoid of reminders of peacetime duties. In the upper left, soldiers stand in formation in front of a local headquarters, which had the German war flag raised outside. Guideposts (upper right) were a distinguishing feature of the German Army in the field and served to orient personnel. Generally, the more signs, the farther from the front one was. Finally, the individual in the tent at left may not have had the luxury of a permanent structure, but he seems to have adapted himself to prevailing conditions fairly well. Note the makeshift lounging chair and writing desk, the washbasin, and what appear to be local melons along the bottom edge of the tent. Given the fact that an operations bus is parked in the background, this living arrangement was probably for a senior officer.

An officer poses for the camera while other officers in the background appear to be in a jovial mood. The device with wires leading to and from it is a switching station for the formation's field telephone network, the *Feldfernsprecher 33*.

The local command appears to have tolerated some humor in its display of guide markers and signs. In this case, the top sign indicates directions to "the ass of the world" (*zum Arsch der Welt*), which was soldier slang for a very remote area, although in this case it may also indicate the local latrine. Despite research, the tactical sign displayed on the next signage cannot be deciphered, although it is clearly for a battalion-level headquarters located at the local military administrative headquarters (*Ortskommandatur*).

A two-man radio team operating a *Torn. Fu. b1* field transceiver from a hastily dug foxhole. The lack of helmets and the relatively shallow nature of their foxhole suggests the battle is moving well ahead of them. While not visible here, the distinctive antenna sticking up from the transceiver made an excellent and sought after target by Red Army snipers, artillery, and aircraft, making the camouflaging of a radio position increasingly important for survival.

A field telephone cable-laying element operating from a specialized vehicle. The field telephone was a reliable means of communication, although the cables themselves were vulnerable to artillery fire if they were not buried deep enough. The landline was the favored means of communication in a static situation since it was impossible to intercept unless directly tapped.

Soldiers are decorated with the Iron Cross, Second Class, by their commanding officer. In contrast to many other armies in World War II, the Germans had a myriad of trade, proficiency, and combat-experience badges and medals that were worn on field uniforms. These were intended to promote individual morale and to inspire other soldiers with less experience. There were precise guidelines for the awarding of these badges and medals, and days of combat experience were recorded in a soldier's field "passport," the *Wehrpaß.*

Several soldiers find time to chat with the local female population. During the opening stages of Barbarossa, German formations were greeted with open arms by the local populace, especially in the Ukraine. The lead truck in the background seems to have a German flag on its cab. The flags served as aerial identification markers for the *Luftwaffe.*

German tank officers confer with their counterparts in the infantry concerning an upcoming operation. Cooperation between the infantry and the *Panzer* troops was usually excellent as a great deal of emphasis was placed on this during training.

A platoon of German infantry–the soldier in the foreground carrying an *MG34* while the man to the right has slung his *MP40*–wait to advance while staring off to the front where the battle rages. Judging by the mosquito netting worn on their helmets, these troops could be near the Pripet Marshes, a massive wetland stretching across part of northwest Ukraine and southern Belarus. Many Red Army soldiers fleeing the German onslaught found refuge in the marshes, which soon became a hotbed for partisan activity against the *Wehrmacht*.

German Army units had cobblers assigned to them to repair footgear and leather items. Since most of the load-bearing equipment of the German Army was manufactured out of leather until well into the war, the unit cobbler served an extremely useful purpose.

A souvenir hunter has scored a Soviet banner.

As Barbarossa wore on and the rainy season arrived, the road network of the Soviet Union was transformed into a sea of mud. These two drivers have taken precautions to help keep them from getting stuck. Both staff cars, adaptations of commercial vehicles and as such not suited to Russian conditions, have had tow cables pre-mounted to the front bumpers of the vehicles. In addition, the car on the viewer's left has wooden blocks under the wheels to allow it to get traction when moving out.

A German mortar team in action with the 8.1cm *GrW 34* (*Granatwerfer 34*—Model 1934 mortar). The mortar provided very effective high-angle fire support for the infantry, and fifty-four of these mortars were allocated to each infantry division, primarily as a battalion support weapon.

A *GrW 34* mortar crew shields itself as a round is fired. Note that two of the crew steady the weapon by holding the bipod legs. This was to keep the mortar from shifting off target in between rounds when it was not on a stabile firing platform.

A 5cm *leGrW 36* mortar team prepares to fire. This mortar was issued to infantry companies and allowed the company commander immediate fire support for his units. Eighty-four of these mortars were allocated to each division. Note the extremely high angle of the firing tube, which allowed support from the weapon virtually right in the thick of the fighting. The rounds were carried in the "suitcases" seen opened here.

Infantry move forward with ammunition canisters for a machine-gun section. The machine gunner is fourth from the left. A *Panzer IV* stands guard.

Judging from the position of the photographer, he felt either safe enough to stand this close to a flamethrower in action—suggesting this was a training exercise—or confident enough that any Soviet soldiers still inside the bunker were long past the point of being able to return fire. At close to eighty pounds, the *Flammenwerfer 35* was heavy and bulky, but its ability to deal with enemy fortifications made it a weight worth carrying.

A motorcycle messenger aboard his BMW R12 confers with a fellow rider. Coming off the assembly line in 1938, BMW would go on to build close to 40,000 of this type before production switched over to the BMW R75 in 1942. Nonetheless, the BMW R12 would soldier on until the end of the war in 1945, serving on every front.

A dust-covered and road-weary *Kradmelder*, a motorcycle dispatch rider, takes a break along a stretch of road. The rapid pace of the German advance, coupled with the relatively short range and temperamental performance of radios, meant that sending messages to and from the rapidly changing front line could be challenging. By utilizing dispatch riders and motorcyles like the DKW 350 pictured here, the Wehrmacht was able to coordinate its units over vast distances in a fairly quick period of time, adding to the awe and terror of *Blitzkrieg*.

German field cemeteries. The Germans marked the location of all dead and then transferred them to cemeteries of the type illustrated here.

Prayer Card
for
Johann Georg Augsberger
Rifleman in a Motorized Reconnaissance Force
son of a farmer from Weiherzant
found a Hero's Death
during an engagement in the East
on 30 June 1941 at the age of 31.

Dearest one, you died a hero's death
for the Fatherland;
with your brave hand
you have gained a place in heaven.

O God, grant him perpetual peace
and may perpetual light shine upon him!
God, let him rest in peace.

Our Father. Ave Maria.

Field burial plots for six soldiers. It was common practice for the soldier's headgear to be placed at the gravesite, as well as a marker indicating the soldier's name, unit, and date of death.

A "tent city" is established in a small Russian village. These tents were intended for four soldiers each (on the basis of one shelter-half per soldier).

Two officers enjoy a meal in the field. They are probably from a light infantry—*Jäger*—unit based on the sleeve insignia on the uniform of the officer on the right. The officer on the left wears a non-regulation plaid shirt under his army sweater.

Three visibly exhausted soldiers take a break. These men are most likely motorcycle messengers, since two of them have report cases *(Meldetaschen)* and one sports a pair of messenger goggles. Note the famous German hobnail boots.

Exhausted soldiers try to sleep while catching a ride.

A machine-gun section takes a breather in the shade of a Russian peasant house. One *MG 34* rests on its bipod, while two more are propped against the side of the house.

Soldiers rest and sleep wherever they happen to drop down during a break in a road march.

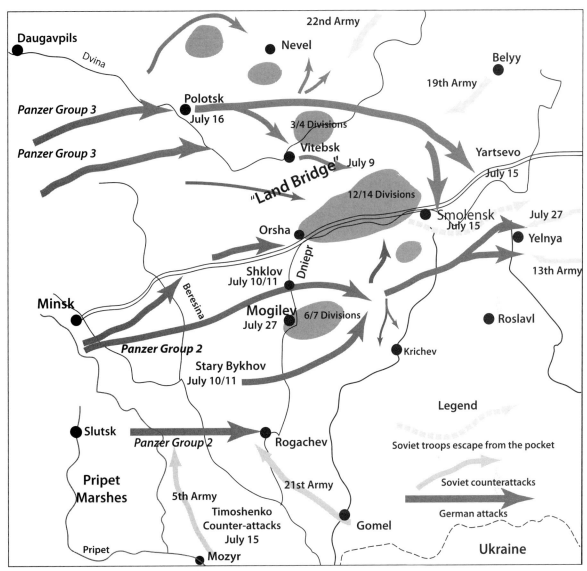

Army Group Center advanced rapidly from Minsk to Smolensk, trapping over 300,000 Soviet soldiers in several pockets. However, Hitler ordered the army group to stop until the ring around Smolensk was completely closed. Fierce Soviet resistance and numerous counterattacks held up the German advance for a crucial two weeks. The drive on Moscow was fatally delayed.

THE SOVIET SOLDIER

Soviet prisioners guarded by a *Panzer II*. The Russian soldier was initially viewed with contempt by his Germans counterpart, but his bravery, fighting ability, and capacity to endure extreme hardship eventually earned their grudging respect. The mass surrenders were not due to cowardice but the dislocation caused by the speed of the German advance. Soviet troops became isolated, without orders and supplies.

One of the captors looks particularly pleased with himself.

Rail transport to prisioner-of-war camps in Poland and Germany.

By September 1941, an estimated 2,000,000 Soviet prisioners had been taken. The German rear-area services were almost completely overwhelmed by these masses of prisioners as no provisions had been made to feed, house, or transport such numbers.

Russian prisoners head to the rear to await an uncertain fate. Masses of Red Army soldiers surrendered in the face of the German advances in 1941, with the German Army logistically unprepared to handle such numbers. The Soviet prisoners were generally treated as well as could be expected under the circumstances, although the war became increasingly brutal on both sides as the German Army was subjected to atrocities committed by the Red Army against German prisoners and wounded. Of the total of 5.7 million Soviet soldiers captured by February 1945, 2.7 million died in German captivity. This was not due to a deliberate policy of extermination but rather a combination of indifference and the inability of the Germans to cope with these masses of prisoners. A shortage of shelter, food, and the spread of infectious diseases, such as typhus, in the camps took a fearful toll of lives. It should be noted that the majority of these deaths occurred prior to the summer of 1942. After then, conditions for the prisioners did improve considerably.

"A broad, earth-brown crocodile slowly shuffling down the road toward us. From it came a subduded hum, like that from a bee-hive. Prisioners of war, Russians, six deep. We couldn't see the end of the column. As they drew near, the terrible stench which met us made us quite sick; it was like the biting stench of the lion house and the filthy odor of the monkey house at the same time." —*Schütze* Benno Zeiser[4]

One of the most notorious German armed forces decrees was the "Commissar Order" of 6 June 1941. This order stated that Soviet army political commisars were not to be taken prisioner but shot, in a clear violation of international law. The conflict in the East was characterized by both sides showing an unprecedented disregard for the widely accepted "rules of war."

Scenes of wrecked Soviet vehicles were common in the first months of the campaign. It is probable that these trucks were destroyed by *Panzers* rather than the *Luftwaffe* due to the absence of bomb craters.

An array of captured Red Army weapons. Included are 45mm antitank guns, heavy machine guns (including a 12.7mm DShK heavy machine gun), and 82mm mortars.

A *Hilfsfreiwilliger*—"volunteer helper"—with his unit. The Hiwis, as they were referred to by the common foot soldier, generally performed rear-area services and tasks, although some actually scouted for the Germans and performed duties in or near the front lines. Most were treated very well by their "sponsor," and great efforts were taken at the end of the war to make sure they did not fall into Russian hands along with German soldiers, since they were often shot out of hand as traitors.

THE GERMAN ENGINEER

The following series of photographs are from an unidentified engineer (*Pionier*) battalion. The engineers had a multitude of essential functions, including road and bridge builders, fortification specialists, mine laying and clearing, and demolition. In addition the engineers were expected to function as combat soldiers, which they did superbly.

In these two photographs, a pass-in-review is conducted on a blustery fall or winter day. The battalion band plays in the background. These were probably taken at the battalion's garrison in Germany.

Eight pontoons of a "Bridge Column B" lined up with their trailers.

With the fall of 1941 came the "mud season" in Russia, turning all unimproved roads into quagmires. Here a motorcycle with sidecar attempts to move up a slope while a broken-down truck waits forlornly in the background.

Artillery fires smoke rounds to cover an impending ground operation. Smoke was primarily used to deny the enemy observation of friendly movement and maneuver.

Engineers move a pontoon section into place for building a bridge. They appear to have adopted a somewhat unconventional uniform to cope with the heat of the Russian summer.

Engineers prepare to finish a bridge parallel to an existing structure on one of Russia's many waterways. While bridges could be captured wholly or partially intact—as the one above apparently was—they often needed to be reinforced or augmented to cover the traffic and logistical needs of a modern army. This bridge is possibly spanning the Beresina River.

Local civilians were often used to assist in projects like this. In this case, a German soldier, possibly an interpreter, talks to who appears to be the Russian foreman.

An engineer observes the work being completed on the original span illustrated above.

Another view of the bridge project. In this image, we see a footbridge being used by a number of Russian civilians.

A "joiner" is used to link two sections of the pontoon bridge.

This photo is particularly interesting as it shows an *Hs 126* single-engine aircraft towing what apperars to be a *DFS 230* glider. The Germans used gliders extensively for delivering essential supplies.

The final span of the bridge is being worked on.

Additional views of the major construction project.

A *Drehkran* six-ton crane, mounted on a truck which has been modified to operate on railway tracks, is used to add spans to a bridge project over what appears to be a railway cut.

Construction of what appears to be a "B Type" bridge with a twenty-ton capacity. The structure is suspended on full pontoons. The roadway consists of wooden planks.`

What appears to be a *Panzer III* crosses the "B Type" bridge. The heaviest German tanks of that period weighed around twenty-three tons, and the reinforced version of this bridge could support their weight.

A member of the battalion has photographed motorized traffic, including some light armor, heading down a dirt road in Russia, sending up telltale signs of dust.

Another "B Type" bridge, in this instance a ten-ton version, suitable for carrying light vehicles and trucks but not heavier armor like the *Panzer III* and *IV* and *StuG III.*

Another job completed, a bridging column moves down the road to its next assignment. A motorcycle messenger looks on.

Members of a unit gather around a staff car to hear an announcement, probably details of the next mission.

This Opel *Blitz* truck has been field-modified to add a permanent structure to its bed. This was often done in the field to make work conditions more bearable for soldiers, especially in maintenance units or staff sections. Note the large amount of equipment on the ground that was probably normally stowed inside the wooden addition.

Another Opel *Blitz*. This one most likely houses a unit's orderly room, as indicated by the banks of binders visible through the opened tarpaulin. The *Blitz* was the most common military truck and had a three-ton capacity.

Engineers take advantage of another day of magnificent weather to finish their light bridge *au naturel*, using the larger version of the pneumatic boat.

The heavy bridge, specifically for armored and heavy vehicles such as this eighteen-ton *FAMO*.

These engineers in waders attempt to finish a bridge in a partially frozen river. The large party of observers may indicate that this is a training exercise.

Once "General Winter" arrived, the German forces found themselves hopelessly ill-prepared to deal with its harsh conditions. While many soldiers had winter uniforms that were suitable for a western European winter, they were inadequate against temperatures that frequently reach 40 or 50 below at nighttime. The situation was mirrored with the equipment as well: antifreeze was insufficiently available or non-existent; breech mechanisms refused to function properly; motor oil virtually solidified. Vehicles had to be run most of the night to keep from freezing over, exacerbating an already critical fuel situation. In time, stop-gap measures were developed that helped tide the Germans over, but there was a crisis in morale that proved almost as difficult to fix.

Soldiers move household items on a *panje* sled. Several have Russian articles of clothing to combat the cold, including a sheepskin overcoat and "commissar" caps. German units quartered in Russian villages as much as possible. Although the conditions in the peasant hovels were frequently miserable—cases of infectious diseases rose dramatically and legions of lice made sleeping almost impossible—the conditions were far better than on the outside. During the defensive fighting that marked the end of Barbarossa, most formations fought for the control of villages in order to have places to house their personnel, and retreating forces often razed villages to deprive the pursuing enemy a chance to spend the night in warm quarters.

Even the sure-footed *panje* horse sometimes had difficulty on the snow and ice, much to the amusement of the soldiers here.

The dead were often left exposed to the elements, the ground frozen too hard to dig burial plots without the use of explosives.

With frequent snowfall, roadways had to be shoveled constantly to maintain an open corridor. Since Soviet snowplows were non-existent and German ones almost as scarce, this meant that soldiers, Hiwis, and Russian civilians had to be employed to shovel snow.

Above and next page top: A column of *panje* sleds moves out into the vast expanse of snow. Movement had to be conducted in groups, not only to make sure that personnel did not become overcome by the elements but also to provide security against the growing menace of partisan attacks. Although not known for certain, this could very well be a combat unit, even a formally motorized one, since the *panje* was often the only way for the Germans to move around the battlefield.

It is not known whether this train derailed as a consequence of partisan action or due to a man-made failure. It appears that at least one of the cars was used for the transportation of wounded (Red Cross markings).

Partisan activity was beginning to be widespread and quite effective by this period of the war. Many of the partisan groups consisted of Soviet soldiers who had chosen to go into hiding rather than surrender. These groups were soon well organized and well supplied. The increasingly tenuous German supply lines were prime targets.

GERMAN MOTORIZED AND ARMORED VEHICLES

A motorized column awaits orders to move out.

Soldiers converse during an impromptu halt. The vehicle is a Horch staff car, the *Kfz. 12*. These personnel cars were based on commercial chassis supplied by various automakers.

A quick meal is taken by the roadside. Trucks were the only effective means of getting supplies, paricularly fuel and ammunition, to the fast-moving, wide-ranging *Panzer* forces. In this case, the Germans have appropriated a Soviet Gaz AAA 1.5-ton 6 x 4 truck.

A support truck fords a shallow waterway. Due to the lack of adequate bridges, fords were also prized discoveries and a high priority target for reconnaissance elements.

Whenever tanks and other armored vehicles appeared on the battlefield, they inspired confidence in the hard-slogging infantry. Usually, they were trailblazers, but armored elements were also frequently called back to open up interdicted lines of communication or to free up foot elements that had been encircled or were encountering resistance greater than they could handle. Here a *kleiner Befehlswagen auf Panzerkampfwagen I*—the small *Panzer I* command and control vehicle—speeds down a roadway. Already obsolescent, the *Panzer I* was still employed in some numbers during Barbarossa, although frequently relegated to scouting and security missions. The *Panzer I* command and control vehicle was eventually replaced by a model based on the *Panzer III* chassis.

A column of armor advancing. These are predominantly *Panzer III's,* the standard German main battle tank of the time. Experience during the Battle of France in 1940, where the more heavily armored and armed Souma S35 and Char B tanks were encountered, demonstrated that a more powerful main gun than the 3.7cm had to be fitted. Adolf Hitler, who liked to dabble in technical details, correctly insisted on the 5.0cm L/60, the most powerful weapon that could be fitted to the *Panzer III* turret. Unfortunately, for cost reasons, the army ordnance office fitted the far less powerful L/42 version that was effective only against the T-34 and KV at pointblank range.

Officers meet during a break in a road march.

A *StuG III Ausf. B* assault gun, a turretless infantry support vehicle based on the *Panzer III* chassis. This vehicle was increasingly used in the antitank role after its introduction in the French campaign in 1940. Despite its low-velocity 7.5cm L/24 gun, the *StuG III* was capable of sucessfully taking on the T-34 and KV, although only at short range. The vehicle's low height made it easier to conceal, and its heavier frontal armor of 5.0 cm made it less vulnerable to tank fire than the *Panzer III*. The top vehicle has also had sections of track applied to the front hull of the vehicle, giving it even greater frontal protection. The soldier on the viewer's right is wearing the distinctive grey double-breasted jacket issued only to assault gun crews.

A *Panzer III* moves down a secondary road in southern Russia, the mountains of the Caucasus in the background. Like the *StuG III* on the previous page, it has also added supplementary armor to the hull in the form of a section of track.

An early version of the standard German Army armored personnel carrier, the *Sd.Kfz. 251*, moves slowly across an engineer pontoon bridge. At the same time, an artillery piece, probably a *10.5-cm leFH 18*, is manhandled since it may have been too unsteady to cross the bridge under tow or the combined weight of the prime mover and the gun was too great for the bridge.

Several *Panzer III's* negotiate some sort of natural obstacle by means of engineer bridging beams. Note the additional items stowed on the back of the trail *Panzer III*, a common practice due to the cramped nature of the fighting compartments. External stowage meant the occasional loss of some items in combat, but it gave the crew greater freedom to move in the fighting compartment, a critical factor in any engagement.

When it comes to mechanical matters, every man is an expert. Mechanics and "advisors" check out the drive train of a *StuG III* that appears to have been under tow.

This image shows a staging area for a *StuG III* unit. Judging by the terrain, probably in southern Russia.

A *Panzer II* moves along a dusty road in the steppes. Although both the *Panzer I* and the *Panzer II* were considered obsolescent in 1941, significant numbers were still employed during Barbarossa as German production could never keep up with the demands of the front. The *Panzer II* had a 2cm semi-automatic cannon and a coaxial machine gun. Like the *Panzer I*, the *Panzer II* had the disadvantage of having a tank commander who was also the vehicle's gunner. The *Panzer II* was primarily used for scouting.

The same type of road as above, only after a rainstorm. With its narrow tracks and relatively high ground pressure, the *Panzer II* could have difficulty in negotiating muddy and snowy ground, especially cross-country. Russian tanks, with their generally wider tracks, were much more suited to the terrain.

A column of *Panzer III's* on the move. During administrative road marches, crewmembers frequently rode on the outside of the vehicle to escape the confines of the cramped interior and to get some fresh air. The short 5.0cm L/42 gun is clearly visible. The "L" refers to the length of the gun in calibers. The L/60 main gun was thus 300 cm in length. The L/42 main gun was 210 cm in length, a substantial difference that significantly affected muzzle velocity and penetrating power.

An early version of the *Panzer IV*, most likely a D or E Model, with the short 7.5cm L/24 main gun. When the Germans entered the war, the *Panzer IV* was the heaviest combat tank in their arsenal and fielded only in limited numbers. By the time of Barbarossa, it was rapidly becoming the mainstay of the *Panzertruppe* and would be produced until the end of the war, with later models fielding a longer, and much more lethal, L/48 7.5cm main gun. In all, more than 8,500 of these tanks were produced by war's end.

Another tank frequently seen during Barbarossa was the *Panzer 38(t)*, which was the German designation for the former Czech tank manufactured by the Skoda factory. When the *Panzer* force was basically doubled in size at the start of the war, German production was not nearly adequate for providing the numbers of tanks needed, and large numbers of these Czech tanks were impressed into German service. Armed with the 3.7cm main gun and with good automotive features, the vehicle suffered from poor armor protection. Despite that, these tanks saw active field service through 1942, and since the basic chassis and running gear were very good, variations of them—such as reconnaissance models, self-propelled antitank guns and artillery, and also the *Hetzer* tank destroyer—saw service through the end of the war.

In the foreground is the formidable-looking eight-wheeled *Sd.Kfz. 231/232* armored car. Armament was a 2cm automatic cannon and a 7.92mm machine gun. Armor was relatively light at 15-mm. Six of these vehicles were issued to the heavy platoon of the armored car squadron of each reconnaissance detachment. A unique feature was the dual-driver system, with a driver both front and rear, which allowed the vehicle to conduct rapid retrograde movements without exposing its rear to the enemy.

Panzer IV's, accompanied by a *kleiner Panzerbefehlswagen I*, deploy across an open field.

A posed image, most likely for home-front consumption. The tankette is an STZ artillery tractor impressed into German service and frequently used for rear-area security duties.

A *Panzer IV* moves across an engineer bridge while a *Panzer III* awaits its turn. Combat vehicles always had the right-of-way when moving toward the front; all other vehicular traffic had to allow them to the front of the line.

An eleven-ton *Sd.Kfz. 7* burns out on a road. It is not known whether this was an on-board vehicular fire or the result of enemy action. The Germans employed half-track vehicles on an extensive scale in a variety of roles.

A *StuG III C* moves at speed down a dusty Russian road. The main gun has a dust cover mounted to keep dirt out of the barrel.

A *Panzer I.* Introduced in 1935 as a training vehicle, this two-man tank was never intended for combat operations and was obsolete by 1939. However, large numbers continued to be employed even into Barbarossa due to the chronic shortage of combat vehicles in the German Army.

Although this image and the one below were probably taken after 1941—based on the camouflage scheme on the trucks—they give a good idea of how much wheeled transport had to be assisted whenever the roads were turned into rivers of mud. A tracked vehicle, possibly a *StuG III*, leads a column of four trucks and a staff car, all of which are interconnected by tow cables. It was only through such methods that the wheeled vehicles, carrying the much-needed classes of supply, could be brought forward in some sectors. Needless to say, such methods diverted combat vehicles from the front and also put tremendous wear and tear on the tracked vehicles, which were not designed to pull such heavy loads.

Rail transport was generally faster and reduced wear and tear on vehicles.

A traffic jam, Eastern Front style! It is interesting to note the wide variety of vehicles, from purpose-built military prime movers to civilian-impressed trucks, horse-drawn wagons of all types, and even a *Gulaschkanone*, the "goulash cannon," which was the term used by the German soldier for the horse-drawn wheeled field kitchen (lower left).

Another column moves down the road, showing good march discipline and vehicular dispersal. A staff car has stopped, possibly to give one of the motorcycle messengers some instructions or receive a report from them.

A *Fi 156 Fieseler Storch* light utility aircraft cruises along a column. These aircraft were frequently used for observation purposes and often dropped messages to commanders on the ground. The "Stork" was used throughout the war for this and many other purposes, including the evacuation of wounded from the battlefield. This aircraft had exceptional short takeoff and landing capabilities.

A wheeled convoy passes a spot on the road that has been listed as "forbidden for tracked and horse-drawn vehicles."

Another view of a column during a march break. The fenders of these vehicles have been painted white to ease identification of them at night when driving under blackout conditions. The unit is a motorized infantry engineer platoon.

A Soviet Stalinetz S-65 tractor impressed into duty by the Germans to pull wheeled vehicles through a muddy section of road. At a little over eleven tons and equipped with a four-cylinder, 65-horsepower engine, the caterpillar-tracked Stalinetz was a useful tool for the Wehrmacht, especially as road conditions deteriorated.

A *StuG III* crew prepares to recover its bottomed-out vehicle from a roadside ditch. Note the open gun-sight port on the superstructure of this early assault gun. The ridges in the channel leading to the port are designed to cause small-arms fire and shrapnel to ricochet away from it.

A *StuG III* appears to be putting on some sort of firing demonstration for interested observers. This was occasionally done when the relatively new weapons system was sent to an infantry formation for the first time so that the foot soldiers could gain an appreciation for the vehicle's capabilities.

The appearance of heavy French and English tanks during the French campaign prompted the Germans to come up with makeshift answers to combat the problem. One solution was the conversion of the obsolescent *Panzer I* into a tank destroyer by the removal of the turret and the mounting of a captured Czech 4.7cm antitank gun. This tank destroyer was designated *4.7-cm PaK(t) auf Panzerkampfwagen 1 Ausf B* and was the first of many tank destroyer designs to make use of obsolete tank chassis—202 were converted from March 1940 to February 1941.

The chassis on which the conversion was based. The elimination of the rotating turret allowed a much larger caliber weapon to be mounted.

A command and control version of the *Sd.Kfz. 251* is halted in an open field. It belongs to a corps headquarters, as indicated by the vehicle's pennant. Motorcycle messengers follow closely behind, awaiting instructions, while a column of tanks passes to the vehicle's left. These vehicles are from *Panzergruppe 3*, commanded by *Generaloberst* Hermann Hoth.

An 8.8cm *Flak 18* with its *Sd.Kfz. 7* towing vehicle. The *Flak 18* weighed seven tons in travelling order. The half-track carried the gun crew of eleven men.

A later-model *Panzer III* moves at speed along the dusty main street of a Russian village. The fine dust caused additional wear on the engines and tracks, and replacement parts were scarce. Additional protection in the form of track sections is evident.

A *Horch Kfz. 12* medium cross-country personnel car. An antitank gun crew poses for a keepsake photograph. Some rudimentary camouflage has been applied to the vehicle's rear, and one of the soldiers has added foliage to his helmet. The towed gun is probably a 3.7cm *Pak 36*.

A column of *Panzer 38(t)* halts for sheduled roadside maintenance. Long road marches caused much wear on the tanks' engines and running gear, and regular maintenance was essential. The vast distances that had to be travelled in the Russian interior caused an alarming reduction in operational vehicles.

A tank company prepares to move by rail. The closest *Panzer 38(t)* is the fourth vehicle of the 2nd Platoon of the 3rd Company of the regiment. The remaining tanks are numbered analogously.

"General Winter" makes his appearance. These *Panzer IIIs* and *Panzer IIs* have added white paint, or whitewash, over the usual *Panzer* grey finish as camouflage.

An *Sd.Kfz. 251* armored personnel carrier from *Panzergruppe Guderian*, indicated by the white G. A squad of eight *Panzergenadiere* could be carried. More than twenty variants of this vehicle were produced, including antiaircraft and antitank models.

Staff personnel from a headquarters section take a break next to their vehicle, a light motorbus converted from a civilian design.

"Hurry up and wait!" This traffic jam does not seem to bother these soldiers too much. The lack of good roads and the fact that most of the German transport was roadbound caused massive traffic-control problems.

This driver and an observer seem to be checking the bridge to make sure the vehicle can cross after an end span girder has broken.

A collection point for worn-out and battle-damaged *Panzer IIIs* and *IVs*. As the invasion wore on, mechanical breakdowns in addition to combat losses took an increasingly heavy toll on German panzer divisions. Compounding the problem, the farther the Germans advanced into the Soviet Union, the more stretched their supply lines became. This would make it impossible to fully supply the *Wehrmacht's* need for fuel, ammunition, spare parts, and new vehicles and weapons. Cannibalizing derelict vehicles for parts to keep the survivors operational became a necessity.

In addition to painting bumpers and fenders for greater recognition during night and limited-visibility operations, this medium open truck has had technical data concerning its length, width, and load capacity painted on the driver cab door.

SOVIET MOTORIZED AND ARMORED VEHICLES

The appearance of the T-34 tank came as a complete surprise and nasty shock to the Germans. With its sloped armor, high-velocity 76.2mm main gun, advanced diesel engine, and wide tracks, which allowed it to easily traverse difficult terrain, the T-34 completely outclassed the main German battle tank, the *Panzer III*. As tank commander Otto Carius of the *20. Panzer-Division* states in *Tigers in the Mud:* "Another event hit us like a ton of bricks: The Russians showed up for the first time with their T-34s! The surprise was complete. How was it possible that those at the 'top' hadn't known about the existence of this superior tank?"

For all its brilliance, the T-34 was not without its faults, such as an unreliable transmission that sometimes literally had to be hammered into gear and a cramped two-man turret that required the tank commander to do double duty as loader. Perhaps even more serious was the fact that most of the tanks did not come equipped with radios, seriously hampering command and control, especially when compared to the Germans, who had radios mounted in all combat vehicles.

These T-34's would no longer be used against the Germans. The top one appears to have bottomed out while attempting to cross this waterway. The bottom one may have been knocked out. Note the soldier holding the 76.2mm main gun round. This was a bigger round than anything mounted in German tanks at the time.

The T-34 above may have been overturned by an aerial bomb. Though the tank appears intact, the concussive blast force needed to overturn a twenty-six-ton tank could very well have been lethal if the crew were inside. The tank below is a T-40, a light amphibious tank with a crew of two. Produced between 1940 and 1941, this particular T-40 rolled off the assembly line before Operation Barbarossa as it still retains the rudders for its propeller.

Initially, the T-34 was encountered in small numbers that made dealing with it somewhat easier. However, larger numbers appeared on the battlefield after September. General Heinz Guderian: "On October 6 our headquarters was moved forward to Sevsk. 4th Panzer Division was attacked by Russian tanks to the south of Mzensk and went through some bad hours. This was the first occasion on which the vast superiority of the Russian T-34 to our tanks became plainly apparent. The division suffered grievous casualties."[5]

Two views of an overturned T-34. This may have occurred when the tank rammed the truck. Such was the confidence that the Red Army tankers had in their T-34's that ramming of vehicles and even tanks, particularly the *Panzer I* and *II*, was relatively common. This particular T-34, with its cast turret and metal "spider wheels," was built by No. 183 Factory in the late fall of 1941.

The heavily armored KV-1 was another unexpected surprise to the Germans. It was slower than the T-34 but more heavily armored with frontal armor of more than 70 mm. As *Leutnant* Helmut Ritgen of *6. Panzer-Division* states after his first encounter with a KV: "That day changed the character of tank warfare as the KV represented a wholly new level of armament, armor protection, and weight."

A knocked-out KV-1E with additional armor bolted to the turret sides. It is likely that this vehicle was destroyed by an 88mm *Flak* as the KV was impervious to the standard *PaK 36* 3.7cm antitank round. The 88mm *Flak* was the only German weapon consistently used in an antitank role that was capable of knocking the turret of a KV-1 off its race. Artillery, such as 10.5cm or 15cm guns, was also capable of doing the same when firing over open sights. A third possibility is a sympathetic explosion caused by the exploding basic load of ammunition after the vehicle was penetrated somewhere by a smaller-caliber round.

Additional views of knocked-out KV-1's, which were just as feared and respected by German tankers as the T-34. *General* Raus relates the the example of a single KV-1 blocking a supply route for over forty-eight hours. The KV resisted attempts to destroy it with a 5.0cm *PaK 38*, tank gun fire, an 88mm *Flak*, and demolition charges placed by an engineer. Finally, eight hits from another 88mm *Flak* destroyed the tank.[6]

A view from the rear of a KV-2, which was armed with a 15.2cm main gun. The turret was much higher than that of the KV-1 and also much slower in traversing, a fact that German tankers could take advantage of when attempting to engage the behemoth. Generally, however, 88mm *Flak* was frequently called up when these were encountered, since only the 88mm round had the capability of penetrating the Soviet tank's thick armor at more than pointblank range.

Additional views of the KV-2, which seemed to have captured the imagination of German soldiers with access to personal cameras. Perhaps this curiosity was piqued by the large-caliber gun, which was the biggest seen on any combat vehicle the Germans had ever encountered. The KV-2 was an artillery support vehicle, and its massive 15.2cm high-exposive round had a devestating effect.

The KV-2 held a fascination for German troops that was out of proportion to its actual effectiveness on the battlefield. The KV 2 was lumbering, cumbersome and with a slow rate of fire.

Captured KV-2's at a railway siding overrun by German troops as the tanks were in the process of being unloaded

The
COLOR
of WAR

THE WEHRMACHT

Officer's M36
Field Tunic

Soldier's M36
Field Tunic

Standard Steel Helmet

M37 Feldmütze
Officer's Field Cap

Soldier's M34
Overseas Cap

Iron Cross, 2nd Class

Infantry Assault Badge

Wound Badge
Silver—3 Wounds

Soldier's Identity Disc

M1931 Bread Bag

Soldier's Personal Items

Soldier's Pay and
Record Book

M1931 Mess Kit

M35 Map/Dispatch Case

M1931 Canteen
and Cup

Leather
Marching Boots

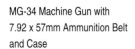

MG-34 Machine Gun with
7.92 x 57mm Ammunition Belt
and Case

Gear and Webbing Harness
Typically Worn by Infantry Soldiers

Tellermine 35 Antitank Mine
with Carrying Case

KAR98k Bolt-Action Rifle 7.92mm

Bayonet and Five-Round
Ammunition Clips

P08 Luger

P38 Walther 9mm

Walther 7.65mm PPK

MP40 with Magazine Pouch
and Luger Holster

KAR98k Ammunition Pouch

Entrenching
Tool

M1928 Stick Grenade

Gas Mask Canister

SSH 39
Combat Helmet

M36 Combat Helmet

M35 Soldier's
Gymnasterka,
Sappers, Infantry

Wrist Compasses

Tanker's Padded
Helmet

Russian Order of
the Red Banner

Soviet Order of the Red Star

ZOMZ 6x Binoculars with Case

THE RED ARMY

Mosin-Nagant Sniper Rifle
7.62mm x 54mm

Mosin-Nagant 7.62mm

RGD-33 Stick
Grenade

RPG-40 Antitank
Grenade

SVT-40 7.62mm

SVT-38 7.62mm

Nagant M1895
Revolver 7.62mm

PPD-34 7.62mm x 25mm

PPSh-41 Submachine Gun
7.62mm x 25mm

M1931 Maxim
Machine Gun 7.62mm

THE PANZERTRUPPEN

Collar Tabs worn
by Panzermen

M38 Officer's Field Cap

Panzer "Wrap" for Officer
in Armored Reconnaissance

Panzer Crash Helmet
with Cloth Beret Covering

THE WAFFEN SS

Runic Collar Tab
Worn on Right Side
of SS Uniforms

M38 "Palm Pattern"
Camouflage Smock

Officer's Field Cap
(missing chin cord)

Officer's M40
Overseas Cap

Steel Helmet

M40 "Palm Pattern"
Camouflage Smock
with Army Splinter
Camouflage Repairs

Two knocked-out or abandoned KV-2s line the street of a Soviet town.

The majority of Soviet tanks encountered during the early days of the campaign were light tanks such as this T-60 armed with a 20mm main gun. Tanks such these and the BT-5, BT-7, and T-26 were easily dealt with by the *Panzer 35* and *38(t)*, *Panzer III* and *IV*, and the *PaK 36* antitank gun.

The BT-5 and BT-7 were encountered in large numbers during Barbarossa. These tanks had the so-called Christie suspension, named after its American inventor, which allowed the vehicle to move with or without tracks. This particular tank may have been set up for high-speed road movement as no tracks can be seen in the photograph.

Another knocked-out or abandoned BT-7, with the so-called "land battleship," a T-35, close behind.

Such was the speed of the German advance that numerous Soviet units were overrun before even deploying for action. This was the case with this trainload of BT-7's with the early-model turret in June 1941 at the beginning of Barbarossa.

Another BT-7 that appears to have been captured intact. The BT series was fast and reasonably well armored for the time and carried a hard-hitting 45mm gun that was superior to the 37mm of the *Panzer 38(t)*. The lack of success was due to the unimaginative, repetitive Soviet tank tactics, compounded by the lack of radios in Soviet tanks.

Additional views of knocked-out or abandoned BT-series tanks. Soviet tank tactics in the early stages of Barbarossa were characterized by haphazard, confused, and piecemeal employment. This allowed the Germans to concentrate superior forces against any armored counterattacks and thereby defeat them.

A captured BT-5 being inspected by a high-ranking officer.

Another light tank encountered in large numbers was the T-26. The T-26 was based on a British Vickers design and saw extensive service not only in the Soviet Union but as an export model throughout the world. Armament is a 45mm tank gun model 32. The T-26 was no match for the majority of German tanks and antitank guns in service at that time.

Behind the T-26 is a massive T-35. The T-35 had five turrets, one housing a 76.2mm main gun, two with 45mm guns, and two with machine guns. The tank was slow and mechanically unreliable and was seen only during the first year of the war in the East. Most of the T-35's were lost to mechanical failure rather than combat action. As only one battalion of T-35s became operational, its appearance on the battlefield was rare.

Three more views (this page and top of next) of the somewhat elusive T-35. The sheer size of the forty-five ton vehicle proved fascinating for German troops. Despite its size, the armor of the T-35 was relatively thin at a maximum of 30 mm.

A T-28 Model 38. Another multi-turreted vehicle, the main turret mounted an L-10 76.2mm gun. The other two turrets mounted machine guns.

The T-28 wieghed twenty-eight tons, and armor on later versions was increased to 50 and 80 mm. Some 400 T-28's were available for action at the start of Barbarossa. Most were lost through mechanical failure.

A knocked-out or abandoned BA-10 armored car. Some 1,200 were in service at the start of Barbarossa and had either a 37mm main gun or 12.7mm heavy machine gun as its main armament. It was largely phased out of service by the end of 1941, although the Germans made extensive use of captured stocks for antipartisan duty in the Balkans.

Artillery spoils of war. A 76.2mm Soviet field gun and prime mover are passed by a despatch rider on a *BMW R75* motorcycle and side-car combination. This field gun was also a highly effective antitank weapon due to its high velocity. The Germans nicknamed it the *Ratsch-Bum* ("Crash-Boom") due to the fact that because of the high muzzle velocity, the sound of the shell exploding preceded the sound of the gun firing.

A quad antiaircraft machine gun comprised of four Maxim machine guns mounted together.

GERMAN AND SOVIET ARTILLERY

A firing battery sets up to fire in the open steppes of Russia. Based on the angle of the gun tubes, these pieces may be firing over open sights. The guns are the standard divisional artillery piece of the time, the 10cm *K18*.

The low elevation of the guns does suggest a direct fire support mission, perhaps even against armor at long range or in support of a tank attack.

The *K18* fired a 33.4-pound shell up to a maximum distance of 20,860 yards. However, the gun was considered somewhat too large and heavy in relation to its caliber.

Gunners take a break and pose for the camera on and around their camouflaged and unlimbered gun. In this instance, a 15cm *K18* howitzer.

The standard German antitank gun at the beginning of Barbarossa, the *3.7cm PaK 36,* was totally useless against the T-34 and KV tanks. It was contemptuously nicknamed by the troops as the "Army Door Knocker" since the only effect it had was for the round to make a noise while bouncing off the Russian armor plate.

Infantry pose with a captured Soviet 85mm antiaircraft gun. Many of these guns were bored out to 88mm in order to accept German ammunition.

Antiaircraft and field guns lie stranded at the river's edge, a testimony to the speed of the German advance.

A detailed view of the quad Maxim antiaircraft machine gun arrangement, mounted on a truck bed.

Divisional artillery goes into position, the prime mover close behind. Note the use of camouflage netting on the *K18*—of doubtful value in such open terrain.

A 10.5cm *le FH 18* field piece is towed through a Russian village. This artillery probably belonged to an infantry division, since the limbers are towed by horses.

The *10.5 cm leichte Feldhaubitze 18* was the standard divisional field howitzer of the German armed forces. The *le FH 18* was a reliable and stable weapon that was easy to handle. However, its maximum range of 11,675 yards fell short of its Russian and British counterparts.

The deadly 88mm *Flak*, possibly deployed here in a field artillery role. An outstanding dual-purpose weapon, its high velocity and flat trajectory made it an ideal antitank gun, despite its large size. During the early stages of the campaign, it was the only weapon capable of destroying the T-34 and KV out to 1,500 meters.

A hastily emplaced 88mm *Flak 36* that has probably been used in the antitank role. The front bogie wheels appear to be damaged, possibly in the haste to position the 88, as indicated by the tire marks off the side of the road.

A crew for a *Flak 36* prepares to move out after limbering up its gun. Note the number of "kill" rings on the barrel. These could be awarded for air or ground targets, but given the large number, they are probably for ground targets.

Far more effective than the *PaK 36* was the *5cm PaK 38*. It was in the process of replacing the puny *PaK 36* at the start of the campaign. This weapon was usually capable of knocking out the T-34 and KV-1 at short and medium combat ranges.

A Soviet 76mm antiaircraft gun being towed by an artillery tractor.

Assorted artillery pieces and their limbers provide more mute testimony to the speed of the German advance, which often overran Soviet emplacements before they could fire a single shot. In the foreground is a 76.2mm Field Gun Model 1936 in an antitank role.

Two 152mm Soviet heavy field guns. The top gun is the M1937 model while the lower photo shows the newer M1938 model capable of firing a heavier shell. Substantial numbers of this excellent weapon were captured in the early stages of Barbarossa and saw large-scale service with German heavy artillery detachments and for coastal defense.

The antiaircraft gun is a Soviet 37mm, based on the Bofors 25mm. Rugged and easy to maintain, it was often employed in the dual-purpose role. Many of the captured guns were converted to German fire control equipment.

An *Sd. Kfz. 7* prime mover and *10cm K18* artillery piece slowly make their way across an engineer bridge.

Gun crews rest or pose for pictures in these two images. In the top image, the letter "C" can be seen behind the gun shield, indicating it is the third gun of the battery, whose pieces were lettered consecutively. In the bottom image, the crew appears to be between firing missions, inasmuch as shells stand ready for loading and mating to charges (wicker holders to the rear of the gun) and the camouflage netting has been moved out of the way.

An excellent firing sequence of a 10.5cm *le FH 16* from an the artillery regiment of an infantry division. This version is designed for horse-drawn, rather than motorized, transport

A 105mm *Flak 38*. This heavy antiaircraft gun was, like the 88mm, supplied with special antitank rounds. However, as this weapon was rarely deployed close to the front lines, it was seldom used in this role.

A gun crew proudly poses around its 2cm *Flak 38*, which appears to have been quite successful in ground combat, given the number of "kills" it has recorded.

The *Flak 38* crew has partially camouflaged its gun position in an open field. Most of the crew have likewise applied some vegetation to their helmets. The degree of camouflage applied was usually directly proportional to the threat from the air.

This 15cm K18 has just finished firing at a distant target. While the smoke from the discharge continues to dissipate, a gun crewman still shields one of his ears.

A 21cm *Mörser 18* is prepared for firing. The heavy gun was used by separate artillery battalions, usually in direct support of corps or field armies. It was transported in two pieces, which were assembled in the field at the designated firing positions. The shell (not counting powder) weighed approximately 250 pounds and was manhandled into the breech by the crew, as seen in this image. It was a unique weapon, featuring a dual recoil system (both gun tube and carriage proper recoiled). It was fielded only in relatively small numbers.

Two variations on moving the *PaK 36:* above, a light one-ton half-track; below, manpower. The soldier on the viewer's left (below) is carrying ammunition in ready-use containers.

A fine shot of a 15cm howitzer at full recoil. The gunner has his mouth open to relieve the air pressure generated by the propellant charge.

The first gun of the light field gun battery, as indicated by the letter "A" on the inside of the gun shield. The crew takes a break between fire missions.

A group photo posed in front of what appears to be a captured Soviet M1910/30 152mm howitzer.

According to *Generaloberst* Erhard Raus, commander of the 4th and 3rd Panzer Armies: "The efficiency of the Russian artillery varied greatly during the various stages of the war. In the beginning it was unable to achieve an effective concentration of fire, and furthermore was unenthusiastic about firing on targets in the depth of the battle position even when there was excellent observation."[7]

An abandoned Soviet 76mm antiaircraft gun on cruciform platform with its fully tracked prime mover.

A Soviet 85mm antiaircraft gun. This weapon was equivalent to the famous German 88mm *Flak 18/36*.

In this photo and the next, a *K18* gun crew relaxes and waits for its next fire mission. Just what has caused the dense column of smoke is unknown, perhaps the result of an airstrike or counterbattery fire. The *sang-froid* of the crew is, nonetheless, quite impressive.

"Our guns began spitting their fire at the town ahead. The first hits we could see; thereafter, everything was clouded in smoke. Flames shot up high in the air; houses must have been burning. Then we saw a huge explosion that looked like a volcano erupting. I guessed we had hit an ammunition dump in town." Werner Adamczyk of the *20. Artillerie Regiment, 20. Panzergrenadier-Division.*[8]

Soldiers take advantage of a lull in the fighting to do laundry and generally attend to personal matters. Such lulls were infrequent but eagerly anticipated by the frontline soldier.

Engineers put the finishing touches to a field-expedient wood-beam bridge.

Giant prime movers such as these twelve-ton *Sd.Kfz. 8.* were needed to tow larger artillery pieces or evacuate/recover heavier armored fighting vehicles.

An *sFH 18* receives a resupply of ammunition. The consumption of rounds by the artillery was enormous and required a huge logistical effort to keep the guns supplied.

ARTILLERY BATTALION 850

The following series of photographs is from an artillery unit: *Heeres Artillerie Abteilung 850*. This was a corps-level unit attached to the 10th Corps of the 16th Army operating with Army Group North. Note the use of an aerial identification marker flag on the hood of the prime mover.

A *Panzer 38(t)* moves past the unit marker sign.

Two officers have the opportunity to take in a relatively relaxed meal, using their staff car as a table. Note the blackout covers placed over the headlights, which allowed only a small beam of light to protrude while driving at night. The officer to the right is a recipient of the Iron Cross, First Class, a relatively rare award this early in the war.

A battery prepares for firing. Some attempt has been made to camouflge the position

Observing targets from a 15cm *sFH 18*

These officers study maps from their staff car, which appears to have some camouflage in the form of vegetation partially placed around it.

While the Maginot and Siegfried Lines are perhaps the most well-known fortified lines of in the Second World War, the Soviets also employed concrete bunkers in defense. In the end, neither the Stalin nor Molotov Line proved effective, although a few individual bunkers were courageously defended.

One of the most important events for a soldier in the field: mail call! The unit first sergeant—identifiable by the two rows of braid worn approximately thirteen centimeters from the bottom of each cuff—distributes the mail to awaiting messengers.

A company or battery commander discusses business with his senior noncommissioned officers, including his first sergeant, standing to the commander's right. Unlike the U.S. Army, most platoon leader positions were NCO's in the German Army. In many an infantry company, there was only one other officer besides the commander, usually a *Hauptmann* or an *Oberleutnant*.

Two soldiers stand guard at the graves of fallen comrades. Whenever possible, formal burial ceremonies were conducted for the fallen, especially in the early years of the war.

The angle of the barrel indicates relatively distant targets, and the camouflage hints at the possibility of Red Air Force activity.

A young *Oberleutnant*, perhaps with an artillery element, takes a moment to pose for the camera in his slit trench.

This page and the next: members of the unit curiously inspect destroyed or abandoned KV-1s. It is possible that the unit may have actually knocked out these vehicles with their field guns while firing over open sights. This is the same KV-1 shown on page 104.

A KV-1 crudely marked with a swastika chalked on to the side of the turret. The protrusion at the rear of the turret is a machine-gun mount.

An award ceremony, most likely for the Iron Cross, Second Class. The German Army established a comprehensive range of awards, recognizing the positive morale effect of recognition for the deeds of the soldiers.

An elaborate gravesite for *Gefreiter* Heinrich Gembs of *2./s.Art.Abt. 850*. The Germans took great care to pay respect to their fallen comrades.

A break is taken at every opportunity.

Once positions had become static and both sides transitioned to a defensive posture, the field fortifications and fighting positions grew ever more elaborate, as evidenced by these images, and almost took on the nature of permanent structures. Given the vegetation and the fact that static warfare developed in the northern theater of operations, that is where these pictures were probably taken.

An officer, probably the battery commander or the battery officer, poses near a camouflaged gun position for a *schwere Feldhaubitze 18*. The shells for the gun are neatly arrayed on top on an ammunition crate, which is labeled for that particular artillery piece: *Kart.s.F.H. 18—Kartusche schwere Feldhaubitze 18*—Cartridge, Heavy Field Howitzer 18.

Three views of the firing positions for this officer's battery.

Two soldiers observe the burnt-out wreck of a Soviet Po-2 biplane. Although completely obsolescent, the inventive Soviets discovered a way to continue to use them rather effectively in the early part of the war: the aircraft were used to fly harassing missions against German lines. Protected by the darkness, the aviators would fly around the battlefield and rear area at relatively low altitude and drop small bombs on anything that looked suspicious. Although they rarely inflicted much in the way of casualties, they were a nuisance and often kept the soldiers on the ground on edge at random times during the night.

A German forward observer in a foxhole with a *Scherenfernrohr SF 14*, a 10-power scissor scope affectionately called "Donkey Ears." The two ocular tubes could be used in either vertical periscope mode, as shown, or laid flat until they were horizontal, allowing the scope to be used in stereoscopic mode for great depth of field.

Gun burst! This *schwere Feldhaubitze 18* has lost most of its gun jacket and tube after a round apparently exploded in the weapon upon ignition. Although most of the force of the blast went downrange, shrapnel could be sent flying anywhere, posing an extreme danger to the gun crew. Despite massive damage, the gun could usually be repaired in the field, as shown in the last picture in this sequence, by replacing the gun jacket and tube, assuming these were on hand.

Daily life for a gun battery in the winter. The howitzers have been given a rudimentary coat of whitewash, since the onset of winter has covered the ground with a blanket of snow. The wicker casings seen being stored in several of the images are storage containers for the shells. In the full-page image on 167, the unit first sergeant reports to the battery commander. In the last image in this sequence, one of the guns appears to have been unlimbered improperly and taken a nosedive into the frozen ground.

Cleaning the barrel, a tedious task at any time, but particularly in these conditions.

The standard German "great coat" was barely adequate for the Russian winter and heavier versions were issued for the winter of 1942. Many officers privately purchsed sheepskin coats. Most of these soldiers are wearing what appear to be felt boots, which were very effective pieces of footwear.

The extent of the German advance by the end of September 1941. German forces are well to the east of the Stalin Line and threatening Moscow. Leningrad is effectively surrounded and under artillery and aerial bombardment but will not be captured.

GERMAN AND SOVIET AIR FORCES

The rugged and agile I-16 *Rata* (Rat) was no match for the standard *Luftwaffe* fighter, the *Bf 109F*. The I-16 had a top speed of 304 miles per hour in contrast to the 390 miles per hour of the *109F*. Despite the initial huge numerical superiority of the Red Air Force with about 8,000 aircraft, the *Luftwaffe*, fielding some 2,800 aircraft, established immediate air superiority.

Even more archaic than the I-16 are these I-15/I-153 "Chaika" biplanes, both being destroyed on the ground as were most of the Soviet aircraft destroyed in the opening stages of the campaign. The I-153 had a top speed of 280 miles per hour and was armed with four 7.62mm machine guns.

The first Soviet aircraft shot down on the first day of Barbarossa was either an I-16 "Rata" by *Oberleutnant* Robert Olejnik at 0340 (or 0358) hours or an I-153 "Chaika" destroyed by *Leutnant* Hans Witzel at 0354 hours, with another I-153 downed less than a minute later.[9]

A shot-down Soviet Tupolev SB-2 twin-engine bomber. The SB-2 was the standard medium bomber of the Red Air Force. It carried a 1,300-pound bomb load at a speed of 279 miles per hour. Defensive armament was a barely adequate four 7.92mm machine guns.

Another view of the SB-2. Although most Soviet aircraft were destroyed on the ground, the *Luftwaffe Bf 109's* took a fearful toll of the usually unprotected attacking formations. On 22 June 1941, *Major* Günther Lutzow's *JG 3* shot down twenty-seven Soviet bombers in fifteen minutes without suffering the loss of a single aircraft.

Red Air Force losses were enormous during the initial stages of the invasion—1,200 aircraft in the first eight hours and 4,600 within a week. Most of these aircraft—3,150—were destroyed on the ground.

Two *Luftwaffe* mechanics take a break on the tail unit of a SB-2. In the foreground is one of the SB-2's V 12 M103 engines of 960 horsepower.

The most devastating weapon the *Luftwaffe* deployed against Soviet airfields was the *SD-2 Splitterbombe*. This was a 4.4-pound fragmentation bomb, fused to explode either on impact or just before. These bombs created havoc amongst rows of parked aircraft as can be seen in these photographs. The *Bf 109* could carry ninety-six of these deadly devices. Although the *Luftwaffe* destroyed large numbers of Soviet aircraft, these were largely obsolete models. The majority of the Soviet pilots survived the initial onslaught. The Red Air Force was crippled but not detroyed.

According to the commander of *1.JG 3, Hauptmann* Hans von Hahn: "We could hardly believe our eyes. Every airfield was chock full of reconnaissance aircraft, bombers and fighters, all lined up in strong straight rows as if on parade. The number of landing strips and aircraft the Russians had concentrated along our borders was staggering."[10]

A Polikarpov PE-2 fast bomber, the Soviet equivalent of the *Junkers Ju88*. The PE-2 was fast, with a top speed of 335 miles per hour, carried a 1,300-pound bomb load, and was well armed with three 12.7mm heavy machine guns and two 7.62mm machine guns.

A totally obsolete TB-3 bomber, the mainstay of the Red Air Force's bomber fleet in the 1930's. The TB-3 lumbered along at 179 miles per hour with its 4,500-pound bombload.

The superb *Bf 109F* *"Friedrich,"* a more powerful and aerodynamically efficient development of the *109*. According to many pilots, a retrograde step was the elimination of the two wing-mounted 20mm cannon of the *Bf 109E*. The F version had a 20mm or 15mm (MG 151) cannon firing through the propeller spinner and two 7.92 machine guns mounted in the engine cowling. The *Friedrich* was vastly superior not only to the I-16 and 1-153 but also to the more modern Yak-1, MiG-3, and LaGG-3 fighters. The latter two lacked maneuverabilty, accelerated sluggishly, and were notoriously difficult to fly. For some unfortunate Soviet pilots, the acronym LaGG stood for *lakirovanny garantirovanny grob*—a "varnished guaranteed coffin." (The LaGG-3 had a highly polished wooden fuselage.)

A *Bf 109E (Emil)*, one of the few *Luftwaffe* casualties of the opening days of Barbarossa. By the evening of June 22, the *Luftwaffe* had lost a total of only thirty-five aircraft. The *109E* was in the process of being repalced by the *F* variant; the remaining *Emils* were increasingly being used as fighter-bombers.

A *Luftwaffe Dornier Do 17P* reconnaissance aircraft has come to grief. *Luftwaffe* reconnaissance aircraft were extremely active in the months before the attack, photographing troop concentrations, airfields, and fortifications on the Soviet western border. On orders directly from Stalin, Soviet fighters and antiaircraft units were stricly forbidden to interfere with these blatant incursions.

A line-up of *Dornier Do 217E* medium bombers. This improved version of the *Do 17* carried a 4,400-pound bomb load at a maximum speed of 273 miles per hour. The *Luftwaffe* was primarily a tactical rather than a strategic force and directly supported the advance of the army. During the opening phase of Barbarossa, this consisted of establishing air superiority by bombing airfields and Red Air Force assembly areas. Cooperation between the *Luftwaffe* and the *Heer* (Army) was excellent as *Luftwaffe* liason officers were attached to all major formations.

A *Heinkel He 111H* medium bomber takes off on another mission. The *He 111*, along with the *Do17/217*, was the standard medium bomber of the *Luftwaffe*, and carried its 4,400-pound bomb load at a maximum speed of 270 miles per hour.

The exceptional *Ju 88* twin-engine medium bomber. An extremely versatile aircraft, the *Ju 88* was used both as a level and dive bomber, a heavy fighter, and, eventually, a night fighter. The Soviet air force had a similar aircraft, the PE-2, which was actually faster than the *Ju 88* but was available only in small numbers in July 1941. The Ju 88 pictured here is adorned with the Edelweiss, the unit symbol for *Kampfgeschwader 51*.

The legendary *Ju 87 Stuka*. Devastatingly effective during the Polish and French campaigns, the *Stuka* myth was shattered during the Battle of Britain, where the *Ju 87* was exposed as slow and extremely vulnerable to fighter attack. However, the *Stuka* gained a new lease on life on the Eastern Front, where, due to *Luftwaffe* air superiority, it initially operated with impunity in daylight.

The crew of a *Ju 87 Stuka* confers with tank crews regarding close support for the advancing *Panzers*. Rugged and reliable, the *Stuka* was an exceptional close-support aircraft, able to deliver its 2,200-pound bomb load with pinpoint precision. The venerable *Ju 87* operated in daylight on the Eastern Front until the last day of the war. The *Luftwaffe* fielded a total of 465 dive-bombers (360 operational), the majority of them *Ju 87*s, on the eve of Barbarossa.

Flying artillery. A welcome sight for the hard-pressed infantry, the *Stuka* provided crucial support in numerous potentially disatrous situations. Even Soviet tanks, like the KV and T-34, were destroyed or put out of action by either direct hits or near misses.

A *Henshel Hs 126B* short-range reconnaissance aircraft has turned over on landing, a not uncommon occurence on the improvised landing strips these aircraft had to use. Each *Panzer* corps was issued its own reconnaissance squadron, thereby ensuring a timely assessment of the tactical situation.

The victim of a landing accident or a raid by Soviet aircraft? Despite the mauling it recived from the *Luftwaffe*, the Red Air Force was still extremely active, launching attack after futile attack with unescorted bomber squadrons. The rigid and predictable nature of these operations led to the slaughter of the attacking aircraft, with entire squadrons being destroyed.

The standard transport aircraft of the *Luftwaffe*—the rugged and reliable tri-motor *Junkers Ju 52*. It was affectionately known to the troops as *Tante Ju* ("Aunt Ju"). In this instance the *Ju 52 is* being used to evacuate seriously wounded soldiers to rear-area hospitals (eleven strecher cases could be carried).

With its three engines, corrugated skin, and fixed undercarriage, the *Ju 52* looked obsolete. However, it was capable of hauling up to 4,000 pounds of cargo or eighteen fully equipped troops at 99 miles per hour. It ranks with the DC3 as one of the greatest of all military transport aircraft.

A *Luftwaffe* ground crew relaxes under the tail unit of a *Do 217*.

THE LAND AND THE PEOPLE

For most Soviet citizens, the promise of a "workers paradise" was not fulfilled. The grinding poverty suffered under the tsars still largely remained, particularly in rural areas.

A destroyed apartment block serves as a backdrop to numerous German sign posts. The frontline troops have moved on, and the occupying forces have arrived. Gottlob Herbert Bidermann, *132. Infanterie-Division*: "Unfortunately, the brutal measures of the Soviets could be compared with the conduct of the German occupiers in the rear areas, far behind the front. Through the excesses that took place against the Russian people, the German soldier became, to the simple Russian, a fighter and supporter against a despised, murderous political institution. Because of this doctrine, established and mandated in far-away Berlin, countless atrocities were in turn committed on soldiers in the front lines."[11]

Among the ruins, the road to Moscow is indicated.

The devastaion of the city area was probably caused by *Luftwaffe* bonbing.

The following sequence depicts the widespread destruction of civilian property. As most of the buildings were of wooden construction, once they caught fire, their total destruction was almost inevitable.

It was not only German bombs and artillery shells that caused these fires. The Soviet forces initiated a deliberate and very effective "scorched earth" policy. Dwellings, barns, bridges, crops, and cattle were destroyed in order to deny them to the German invaders. Seemingly, no thought was given to the effect of this ruthless policy on the civilian population.

This crater was probably caused by a massive aerial bomb, such as a 2,200-pound *SC 1000*.

Local militia assisting in rear-area security against the increasingly strong partisan units.

The grim face of war: civilians forced to evacuate their homes in the wake of combat operations. They were often given only a few minutes to take what pitiful possessions they could carry and leave.

A German mess section feeds some local children. Relations between the frontline soldiers and civilians were generally good. When the rear-area occupying troops took over, the situation was often not so compassionate.

Comfortable quarters for the occupying troops. During the Soviet winter counteroffensive, savage battles were fought for intact villages. The victors had shelter from the cold; the defeated usually froze to death.

Searching for scraps of food from a German supply railway truck. The fate of the Soviet civilian population was particularly tragic as starvation, particularly in the first years of the war, was responsible for millions of deaths.

Even in the midst of combat operations, life must go on for the civilian populace. The alternative was starvation. The Germans were barely able to supply their own troops, much less feed the civilian population.

It is not known whether the widespread destruction of Communist imagery was the result of spontaneous actions of the general populace or deliberate acts by the occupying troops. However, large sections of the populace were not sorry, at least at first, to see the end of Communist rule. Unfortunately, the truth soon became evident that one cruel despot had been exchanged for another.

Many Soviet civilians, particularly in the Ukraine, greeted the German troops as liberators from the oppressive yoke of Communism. Unfortunately, their hopes were ill-founded as the short-sighted and equally oppressive policies of the occupiers became apparent. Potential allies then became partisans.

Examples of the grinding poverty endured by most of the rural population. Images such as these were used by the Nazi propaganda machine to falsely portray the German invasion as a crusade against the evils of Communism.

A study in contrasts: elaborate architecture from the tsarist era and the life of a nomadic cattle herder in the Caucasus.

Female Red Army soldiers. More women saw duty in the military in the Soviet Union than in any other country in World War II. Eventually, some 800,000 were called to duty. While many performed the administrative and medical tasks that were the hallmark of female auxiliaries in most other countries, some saw active combat and were employed with frontline forces. German memoirs are filled with accounts of female soldiers encountered in the front lines and the reluctance with which they were engaged once it was determined they were female.

Civilians suspected of collaborating with Soviet forces were dealt with ruthlessly under martial law and often put on display as a warning to other potential sympathizers.

Heavy-handed administration by rear-area occupying forces only added to the partisan problem. Savage reprisals and mass executions were commonplace and usually counterproductive.

When the German forces hit the pre-1939 Soviet frontier after the start of the invasion, they encountered the Stalin Line, a series of fortified zones that had been built to protect the western frontier of the country. Work had started in 1920 and continued until the signing of the German-Soviet Non-Aggression Pact in 1939 and 1940, when work was started on a new line of fortifications—the Molotov Line—farther to the west to coincide with the territory seized in the wake of Soviet expansion into Poland, the Baltics, and Bessarabia. By the time the Germans ran into the Stalin Line, much of it was rendered indefensible because the weaponry used in the fortifications had been shipped west to be installed in the Molotov Line. Nonetheless, resistance was frequently encountered and, when coupled with fully manned and gunned fortifications, proved to be a formidable nut to crack.

A German notice printed in Russian and Ukrainian handed out in and around Kiev on September 28, 1941. It reads: "All Jews living in the city of Kiev and its vicinity must come to the corner of Melnikova and Dokhturovska Street by eight o'clock on the morning of Monday, September 29th, 1941. They are to bring documents, money, valuables, as well as warm clothes, underwear, etc. Any Jews not carrying out this instruction and who are found elsewhere will be shot. Any civilian entering apartments left by the Jews and stealing property will be shot." The Jewish civilians would be led to the Babi Yar ravine, where over 33,000 would be murdered.

Все жиды города Киева и его окрестностей должны явиться в понедельник 29 сентября 1941 года к 8 часам утра на угол Мельниковой и Доктеривской улиц (возле кладбищ).

Взять с собой документы, деньги и ценные вещи, а также теплую одежду, белье и пр.

Кто из жидов не выполнит этого распоряжения и будет найден в другом месте, будет расстрелян.

Кто из граждан проникнет в оставленные жидами квартиры и присвоит себе вещи, будет расстрелян.

Наказується всім жидам міста Києва і околиць зібратися в понеділок дня 29 вересня 1941 року до год. 8 ранку при вул. Мельника — Доктерівській (коло кладовища).

Всі повинні забрати з собою документи, гроші, білизну та інше.

Хто не підпорядкується цьому розпорядженню буде розстріляний.

Хто займе жидівське мешкання або розграбує предмети з тих мешкань, буде розстріляний.

As a central tenet of Nazi ideology, *Lebensraum*—"living space"—was to be found and taken in the East. The land would be repopulated with Germans and people of Germanic ethnicity while those already living there would be relocated. In the case of the Jewish population, however, a far worse fate awaited them. In this photo, a group of Jewish men, women, and children is herded into a ravine prior to being executed as the Holocaust grows in scale with Operation Barbarossa. As the *Wehrmacht* pushed the Red Army farther east, mobile killing units known as *Einsatzgruppen*—often aided by the *Wehrmacht* as well as by civilians from the conquered lands—systematically rounded up and killed Jewish civilians by the tens of thousands.

APPENDIX

Rank Comparisons

U.S. ARMY	RUSSIAN ARMY	WAFFEN-SS	GERMAN ARMY
Enlisted Men			
Private	Krasnoarmeyets	*SS-Schütze*	*Schütze*
Private First Class		*SS-Oberschütze*	*Oberschütze*
Corporal	Mladshiy Serzhant	*SS-Sturmmann*	*Gefreiter*
Senior Corporal		*SS-Rottenführer*	*Obergefreiter*
Staff Corporal		*SS-Stabsrottenführer*	*Stabsgefreiter*
Noncommissioned Officers			
Sergeant	Serzhant	*SS-Unterscharführer*	*Unteroffizier*
		SS-Scharführer	*Unterfeldwebel*
Staff Sergeant		*SS-Oberscharführer*	*Feldwebel*
Sergeant First Class	Starshiy Serzhant	*SS-Hauptcharführer*	*Oberfeldwebel*
Master Sergeant		*SS-Sturmscharführer*	*Hauptfeldwebel*
Sergeant Major	Starshina		*Stabsfeldwebel*
Officers			
Second Lieutenant	Mladshiy Leytenant	*SS-Untersturmführer*	*Leutnant*
First Lieutenant	Leytenant	*SS-Obersturmführer*	*Oberleutnant*
Captain	Kapitan	*SS-Hauptsturmführer*	*Hauptman*
Major	Major	*SS-Sturmbannführer*	*Major*
Lieutenant Colonel	Podpolkovnik	*SS-Obersturmbannführer*	*Oberst Leutnant*
Colonel	Polkovnik	*SS-Standartenführer*	*Oberst*
Brigadier General		*SS-Brigadeführer*	*Generalmajor*
Major General	General Major	*SS-Gruppenführer*	*Generalleutnant*
Lieutenant General	General Leytenant	*SS-Obergruppenführer*	*General der Fallschirmjäger, etc.*
General	General Armii	*SS-Oberstgruppenführer*	*Generaloberst*
General of the Army	Marshal Sovetskogo Souza	*Reichsführer-SS*	*Feldmarschall*

NOTES

1. H. R. Trevor-Roper, *Hitler's War Directives, 1939–1945* (London: Pan, 1966).
2. Robert J. Kershaw, *War without Garlands:Operation Barbarossa, 1941/1942* (Shepperton, England: Ian Allan, 2000).
3. Ibid.
4. Ibid.
5. General Heinz Guderian, *Panzer Leader* (London: M. Joseph, 1952).
6. Peter G. Tsouras, ed., *Panzers on the Eastern Front: General Erhard Raus and His Panzer Divisions in Russia, 1941–1945* (London: Greenhill, 2006).
7. Peter G. Tsouras, ed., *Fighting in Hell: The German Ordeal on the Eastern Front* (London: Greenhill, 1995).
8. Werner Adamczyk, *Feuer! An Artilleryman's Life on the Eastern Front* (Wilmington, NC: Broadfoot, 1992).
9. John Weal, *Bf 109 Aces of the Eastern Front* (Oxford, England: Osprey, 2001).
10. Ibid.
11. Gottlob Herbert Bidermann, *In Deadly Combat: A German Soldier's Memoir of the Eastern Front* (Lawrence, KS: University Press of Kansas, 2000).

SELECT BIBLIOGRAPHY

Adamczyk, Werner. *Feuer! An Artilleryman's Life on the Eastern Front.* Wilmington, NC: Broadfoot, 1992.

Angolia, John R., and Adolf Schlicht. *Uniforms and Traditions of the German Army, 1933–1945.* San Jose, CA: R. J. Bender, 1984.

Bernage, Georges, and Francois de Lannoy. *Les divisions de l'Armee de Terre allemande: Heer, 1939–1945.* Bayeux, France: Editions Heimdal, 1997.

Bidermann, Gottlob Herbert. *In Deadly Combat: A German Soldier's Memoir of the Eastern Front.* Lawrence, KS: University Press of Kansas, 2000.

Bock, Fedor von. *The War Diary, 1939–1945.* Atglen, PA: Schiffer, 1996.

Buchner, Alex. *The German Infantry Handbook, 1939–1945: Organization, Uniforms, Weapons, Equipment, Operations.* West Chester, PA: Schiffer, 1991.

Burdick, Charles, and Hans-Adolf Jacobsen, eds. *The Halder War Diary, 1939–42.* Novato, CA: Presidio Press, 1988.

Carell, Paul. *Hitler's War on Russia: The Story of the German Defeat in the East.* London: Harrap, 1964.

Chamberlain, Peter, and Hilary Doyle. *Encyclopedia of German Tanks of World War Two.* London: Arms and Armour Press, 1978.

Ellis, Chris, ed. *Directory of Wheeled Vehicles of the Wehrmacht, 1933–45.* London: Ducimus Books, 1974.

Ericson, John. *The Road to Stalingrad.* New York: Harper & Row, 1975.

Gander, Terry, and Peter Chamberlain. *Small Arms, Artillery, and Special Weapons of the Third Reich.* London: Macdonald and Jane's, 1978.

Gooch, John, ed. *Decisive Campaigns of the Second World War.* London: F. Cass, 1990.

Guderian, Heinz. *Panzer Leader.* London: M. Joseph, 1952.

Hardesty, Von. *Red Phoenix: The Rise of Soviet Air Power, 1941–1945.* Washington, DC: Smithsonian Institution Press, 1982.

Hogg, Ian V. *German Artillery of World War Two.* London: Arms and Armour, 1975.

Kershaw, Robert J. *War without Garlands: Operation Barbarossa, 1941/1942.* Shepperton, England: Ian Allan, 2000.

Knappe, Siegfried, and Ted Brusaw. *Soldat: Reflections of a German Soldier, 1936–1949.* New York: Orion Books, 1992.

Lucas, James. *War on the Eastern Front, 1941–1945: The German Soldier in Russia.* London: Jane's, 1979.

Metelmann, Henry. *Through Hell for Hitler.* Havertown, PA: Casemate, 2001.

Murray, Williamson. *The Luftwaffe, 1933–1945: Strategy for Defeat.* Washington, DC: Brassey's, 1996.

Niehorster, Leo W. G. *German World War II Organizational Series,* vol. 3/II, *Mechanized GHQ Units and Waffen SS Formations (22 June 1941).* Milton Keynes, England: The Military Press, 2005.

Porter, David. *Red Army in World War II.* London: Amber Books, 2009.

Research Institute for Military History. *Germany and the Second World War*, vol. 4, *The Attack on the Soviet Union*. Oxford, England: Clarendon Press, 1998.

Smith, J. R., and Anthony Kay. *German Aircraft of the Second World War*. London: Putnam, 1972.

Stahlberg, Alexander. *Bounden Duty: The Memoirs of a German Officer, 1932–45*. London: Brassey's, 1990.

Trevor-Roper, H. R. *Hitler's War Directives, 1939–1945*. London: Pan, 1966.

Tsouras, Peter G., ed. *Fighting in Hell: The German Ordeal on the Eastern Front*. London: Greenhill, 1995.

———. *Panzers on the Eastern Front: General Erhard Raus and His Panzer Divisions in Russia, 1941–1945*. London: Greenhill, 2006.

U.S. War Department. *Handbook on German Military Forces*. Baton Rouge, LA: Louisiana State University Press, 1990.

Warlimont, Walter. *Inside Hitler's Headquarters, 1939–45*. New York: Praeger, 1964.

Weal, John. *Bf 109 Aces of the Eastern Front*. Oxford, England: Osprey, 2001.

Zaloga, Steven J., and James Grandsen. *Soviet Tanks and Combat Vehicles of World War Two*. London: Arms and Armour Press, 1984.

———. *The Eastern Front: Armour, Camouflage, and Markings, 1941 to 1945*. London: Arms and Armour, 1983.

ACKNOWLEDGMENTS

The following people deserve credit for their generous assistance in supplying period photographs taken by the combatants themselves, along with modern color images of uniforms, equipment, and weapons. In each and every case, they went above and beyond to help bring this book to life by offering their expertise and time: Pat Cassidy, Steve Cassidy, P. Whammond and Carey of Collector's Guild (www.germanmilitaria.com), Jim Haley, David A. Jones, Jim Pool, Scott Pritchett, and Aleks and Dmitri of Espenlaub Militaria (www.aboutww2militaria.com and www.warrelics.eu/forum), as well as the National Archives, the Swedish Army Museum, and a few individuals that wish to remain anonymous.